THE
5-MINUTE
SALAD
LUNCHBOX

THE
5-MINUTE
SALAD
LUNCHBOX

HAPPY, HEALTHY & SPEEDY
SALADS TO MAKE
IN MINUTES

ALEXANDER HART

Smith
Street
Books

CONTENTS

INTRODUCTION

~~~~~~

Lunch is a fickle thing. Throughout the working week, any second of spare time is a precious commodity. Prepping lunches in advance can often land at the bottom of your priority list, especially when you're racing out the door to get to work. You end up buying a takeaway lunch every day, which is rarely healthy or worth the collective price tag. If any of this sounds familiar, it's probably time to start packing your own lunchbox. The good news? It doesn't have to be a chore.

These speedy salads are designed to be made before work and will remain crisp and fresh until lunchtime. Keeping the dressing separate is the key to maintaining a fresh crunchiness. Soggy salads are not your friend, so find yourself a lunchbox with a dedicated dressing container or use a small jar.

Using the 52 recipes in this book, you'll be equipped with lunch ideas for every week of the year. Most of the salads can be made from scratch in 5 minutes, while others make the most of repurposing last night's leftovers into a healthy and delicious lunch. Either way, these simple salads will be better tasting and more nutritious than your nearest takeaway lunch option.

Even better, this book is loaded with low-carb and wholegrain recipes that are built around a central protein and lots of fresh produce, so you'll be returning to your desk feeling satisfied and revitalised.

The chapters that follow separate the recipes into five handy categories: Vegetables; Noodles and Zoodles; Grains and Seeds; Beans and Legumes; and Classics and New Classics. When your well of lunch-inspiration has run dry, just flick to your favourite genre of salad and find something to prepare for tomorrow. If you've found a salad that really tickles your fancy, double or triple the quantities in the recipe and eat it throughout the week. You'll be thanking yourself each day.

There's one last thing. Whenever possible, try and step away from your desk for lunch. There is one energy boost that no salad can ever provide: fresh air. Maybe you only have 20 minutes to spare, but if the weather permits then take that time to step out of the office and find yourself a spot that feels quiet and comfortable. Make your lunch break a moment of respite, not just another task to juggle between emails. It is a break, after all.

SALAD INGREDIENTS

Here are a few notes on some of the ingredients used in this book, along with tips and tricks to help cut down your prep time even further.

BEETROOT

Cooked beetroot (beets) are available from the supermarket, usually found in a vacuum-sealed packet for the larger variety and in jars for baby beetroot. Mix it up and use golden or target beetroot when they're in season.

CHEESE

Good-quality hard cheeses, such as parmesan and pecorino, can be purchased shaved, grated or shredded, and crumbled feta is available in tubs in the refrigerated section of your supermarket.

COOKED CHICKEN

Shredded cooked chicken is available from your supermarket deli. Alternatively, buy or cook a whole roast chicken, chop or shred the meat yourself and store in an airtight container in the fridge for up to 4 days. Another healthy option (if you have time) is to poach some chicken breasts for use throughout the week.

CORN

The recipes call for tinned sweet corn; however, if you have more time, chargrill a fresh corn cob instead. Slice off the kernels and add to your lunchbox with the remaining salad ingredients. Alternatively, you can cook the corn ahead of time and keep the kernels in an airtight container in the fridge for up to 3 days.

DRESSING

For most of the recipes in this book, the dressing is kept separately so you can dress your salad just before you eat it. You can save yourself some more time in the morning by mixing your dressing the night before and keeping the container in the fridge – you could even prep a whole week's worth in advance.

HARD-BOILED EGGS

Make a batch ahead of time and keep in the fridge for up to 1 week. To prepare, place your eggs in a saucepan and cover with cold water. Bring to the boil over medium–high heat, then cover, remove from the heat and set aside for 8–11 minutes (depending on how hard you like them). Drain, cool in iced water and peel just before adding to your salad.

HERBS

To save time, chop all of your fresh herbs together.

MINCED GARLIC AND GINGER

Available in jars – or tubes (usually sold as 'paste') – from the supermarket, these really are a time-saving wonder. Alternatively, you can make your own: blitz a large quantity of garlic or fresh ginger in your food processor with a little water, salt and a drop of oil. It will keep well in an airtight container in the fridge for up to 2 weeks, or press flat in a zip-lock bag and store in the freezer for up to 2 months.

POMEGRANATE

The recipes call for frozen pomegranate seeds for the sake of convenience, but you can definitely use fresh seeds if you have them. To save some prep time, remove the seeds from the pomegranate and store in an airtight container in the fridge for up to 3 days.

PRE-CUT VEGETABLES

Supermarkets now carry a large range of packaged pre-cut vegetables that keep really well in your fridge, which is what we recommend using to keep your prep time to around 5 minutes. Look out for broccoli or cauliflower 'rice'; shredded carrot, cabbage and lettuce; spiralised zucchini / courgettes (zoodles) and beetroot (beets); and other convenient combination products, such as coleslaw and mixed salad leaves.

ROAST BEEF

Purchase sliced roast beef from your supermarket deli, or use leftovers if you have them.

TOASTED NUTS & SEEDS

Toast nuts and seeds ahead of time, leave to cool completely and store them in an airtight container in your pantry for up to 1 month.

GRAINS & NOODLES

Bulgur

The recipes in this book allow bulgur to soak and 'cook' in the time between preparing your salad in the morning and eating it at lunchtime. If you have time to prep the night before (and you'd rather not take an extra jar with you), make the bulgur according to the packet instructions and store in an airtight container in the fridge for up to 4 days.

Quinoa & brown rice

There are various 'quick' and 'instant' quinoa and brown rice products available that are ready in 2–3 minutes. Cook according to the packet instructions and allow to cool. Alternatively, if you have time to prep regular quinoa or brown rice ahead of time, cook a large batch according to the packet instructions, then cool and store in an airtight container in the fridge for up to 4 days. Even easier, make enough for leftovers when cooking quinoa or brown rice for dinner, then simply toss with the remaining salad ingredients in the morning. If you can, try using a combination of red and white varieties of quinoa to mix things up a little.

Soba noodles

Cook according to the packet instructions. Rinse well under cold water and drain.

Instant (ramen) noodles

Check the packet instructions, but these should cook in boiling water in 2–3 minutes. Rinse under cold water and drain.

Vermicelli noodles

To prepare vermicelli noodles, place in a bowl and cover with boiling water and allow to sit for 4–5 minutes, giving them a bit of a stir occasionally to loosen them. Rinse under cold water and drain.

NOTES ON QUANTITIES

We find you rarely need exact quantities when putting together a salad, so we've used 'handfuls of' in many cases, making ingredients quick to throw in. Feel free to adjust the quantities to make use of what you might already have in your fridge.

All tablespoons are 15 ml (½ fl oz).

VEGE-
TABLES

BABY BEETROOT, WALNUT & RICOTTA SALAD

The nutty earthiness of baby beetroot (beets) is perfect in this salad, but you can use any roast veggies here. Look for good-quality fresh ricotta, or use goat's curd or Persian feta instead.

◇◇◇◇◇◇◇◇◇◇

50 g (1¾ oz) ricotta

200 g (7 oz) cooked baby beetroot (beets), quartered

2 large handfuls of baby English spinach leaves

¼ red onion, thinly sliced

50 g (1¾ oz) toasted walnuts, roughly chopped

DATE DRESSING

1 medjool date, pitted and finely chopped

2 teaspoons honey

1 tablespoon white wine vinegar

2 tablespoons extra virgin olive oil

salt and freshly ground black pepper, to taste

1 Spoon the ricotta into a small, airtight container.

2 Toss the remaining salad ingredients together, then tip into your lunchbox.

3 Combine the dressing ingredients in a small jar or container with a tight-fitting lid.

4 Pour the dressing over the salad just before serving and toss well. Dot the ricotta over the top and serve.

BROCCOLI RICE, CARROT & CRANBERRY SALAD WITH BUTTERMILK DRESSING

To make this recipe super fast, use pre-cut broccoli and carrots, and use a good-quality store-bought buttermilk ranch dressing, or make the dressing a day ahead.

½ head of broccoli, blitzed to coarse grains or use store-bought broccoli 'rice'

handful of shredded carrot

¼ red capsicum (bell pepper), diced

¼ red onion, thinly sliced

3 tablespoons slivered almonds

2 tablespoons dried cranberries

handful of rocket (arugula)

BUTTERMILK DRESSING

2 tablespoons buttermilk

1 tablespoon Greek yoghurt

juice of ½ lemon

¼ teaspoon minced garlic

salt and freshly ground black pepper, to taste

1. Toss the salad ingredients together, then tip into your lunchbox.

2. Combine the dressing ingredients in a small jar or container with a tight-fitting lid.

3. Pour the dressing over the salad just before serving and toss well.

FENNEL & RADICCHIO CITRUS SALAD

This is a fantastic winter salad. Try this recipe using blood oranges when they're in season. You can save some time in the morning by cutting the orange and fennel the night before – the juice from the segmented orange will help prevent the ingredients from oxidising.

1 orange

½ small fennel, shaved

¼ small radicchio, shaved

¼ red onion, thinly sliced

handful of pitted black olives

50 g (1¾ oz) toasted walnuts, roughly chopped

small handful of parsley, roughly chopped

CITRUS DRESSING

juice of ½ orange

2 teaspoons red wine vinegar

1 teaspoon honey

1 teaspoon dijon mustard

2 tablespoons extra virgin olive oil

salt and freshly ground black pepper, to taste

1. Segment the orange over a bowl to catch the juice. Add the segments along with the fennel and toss to combine.

2. Toss through the remaining salad ingredients, then tip into your lunchbox.

3. Combine the dressing ingredients in a small jar or container with a tight-fitting lid.

4. Pour the dressing over the salad just before serving and toss well.

KOREAN BIBIMBAP SALAD WITH KIMCHI DRESSING

This recipe uses shredded cabbage as the base for a lighter take on the Korean rice-bowl classic. The kimchi dressing gives this salad a real kick – feel free to increase the quantity if you like it hot.

100 g (3½ oz) shredded white cabbage (or use a mix of red and white)

large handful of shredded carrot

1 Lebanese (short) cucumber, diced

1 spring onion (scallion), thinly sliced

1 tablespoon toasted sesame seeds

small handful of bean sprouts

1 hard-boiled egg, cut into wedges

KIMCHI DRESSING

30 g (1 oz) kimchi, roughly chopped

1 teaspoon caster (superfine) sugar

1 tablespoon rice wine vinegar

1 teaspoon sesame oil

1½ tablespoons grapeseed or other neutral-flavoured oil

1 Spread the cabbage over the base of your lunchbox and top with the other salad ingredients.

2 Combine the dressing ingredients in a small jar or container with a tight-fitting lid.

3 Pour the dressing over the salad just before serving and toss well.

RAW BRUSSELS SPROUTS WITH PEAR, HAZELNUTS & PECORINO

The sweetness from the pear and cranberries (also known as craisins) are the perfect foil for the peppery bite of the raw brussels sprouts. Apple will work just as well as pear and, while the hazelnuts bring something really special to this salad, walnuts are great here, too.

150 g (5½ oz) brussels sprouts, shredded

1 pear, thinly sliced

30 g (1 oz) roasted hazelnuts, roughly chopped

30 g (1 oz/⅓ cup) grated pecorino

2 tablespoons dried cranberries

small handful of parsley, roughly chopped

CIDER VINEGAR DRESSING

2 teaspoons dijon mustard

1 teaspoon honey

1½ tablespoons apple cider vinegar

2 tablespoons extra virgin olive oil

salt and freshly ground black pepper, to taste

1 Toss the salad ingredients together, then tip into your lunchbox.

2 Combine the dressing ingredients in a small jar or container with a tight-fitting lid.

3 Pour the dressing over the salad just before serving and toss well.

LEFT-OVER ROAST VEGETABLE SALAD

When I'm cooking roast vegetables for dinner, I always make sure I cook extra, so I'm guaranteed leftovers to use in my lunch the next day. Substitute toasted pine nuts or almonds if you don't have cashew nuts.

◇◇◇◇◇◇◇◇◇◇

200 g (7 oz) left-over roast vegetables, such as carrot, pumpkin (winter squash), parsnip, potato, sweet potato and beetroot (beets), sliced or cut into bite-sized pieces

2 large handfuls of baby English spinach leaves

small handful of parsley leaves, roughly chopped

30 g (1 oz) cashew nuts, roughly chopped

2 teaspoons sumac

TAHINI DRESSING

1 teaspoon minced garlic

2 tablespoons tahini

juice of ½ lemon

1 tablespoon water

salt and freshly ground black pepper, to taste

1. Toss the salad ingredients together, then tip into your lunchbox.

2. Combine the dressing ingredients in a small jar or container with a tight-fitting lid.

3. Pour the dressing over the salad just before serving and toss well.

SOM TUM

A Thai staple, som tum is fresh and big on flavour.
Adjust the amount of chilli depending on how hot you
like it. If you want a really quick option, look for pre-
made som tum dressing at your local Asian grocer.

◇◇◇◇◇◇◇◇◇◇◇

2 red bird's eye chillies (deseeded if you prefer less heat)

2 garlic cloves

1 tablespoon dried shrimp

1½ tablespoons roasted unsalted peanuts

1 tablespoon grated palm sugar

2 tablespoons fish sauce

juice of 1 lime, plus extra wedges to serve

½ small green papaya, shredded

3 snake (yard-long) beans, chopped into 2 cm (¾ in) lengths

large handful of grape (baby plum) tomatoes, halved

1 Pound the chilli and garlic using a mortar and pestle, add the dried shrimp and peanuts and pound until you have a rough paste.

2 Stir in the palm sugar, fish sauce and lime juice.

3 Toss the remaining ingredients together, mix through the dressing, then tip into your lunchbox.

SPRING VEGETABLE SALAD WITH LEMONY RICOTTA

This salad is best made in spring when asparagus and peas are crunchy and sweet. If the peas are really fresh, you can leave them raw. Alternatively, blanch frozen peas if fresh peas are not in season. Use good-quality ricotta from the deli, rather than the packaged kind, as you want it to have a lovely creamy texture.

zest of ½ lemon

50 g (1¾ oz) ricotta

pinch of salt

½ bunch baby asparagus, woody ends trimmed, halved

60 g (2 oz) shelled fresh peas

large handful of snow peas (mangetout), halved lengthways

large handful of sugar snap peas

small handful of mint leaves

HONEY–MUSTARD DRESSING

juice of 1 lemon

1 teaspoon dijon mustard

1 teaspoon honey

2 tablespoons extra virgin olive oil

salt and freshly ground black pepper, to taste

1. Combine the lemon zest, ricotta and salt in a small, airtight container.

2. Blanch the asparagus and peas in salted boiling water for 2 minutes. Drain and refresh under cold running water. Tip into your lunchbox and mix in the remaining salad ingredients.

3. Combine the dressing ingredients in a small jar or container with a tight-fitting lid.

4. Pour the dressing over the salad just before serving and toss well. Dot the lemony ricotta over the top and serve.

SHREDDED BEETROOT, DILL & MUSTARD SEED SALAD

You can usually buy pre-shredded beetroot (beet) from the supermarket to save on your prep time. Feel free to use a mix of different salad leaves, including rocket (arugula), sorrel, soft lettuce leaves and baby English spinach.

200 g (7 oz) shredded raw beetroot (beet)

large handful of dill, roughly chopped

2 tablespoons mustard seeds, toasted

large handful of mixed salad leaves

LEMON DRESSING

juice of ½ lemon

2 tablespoons extra virgin olive oil

salt and freshly ground black pepper, to taste

1 Toss the salad ingredients together, then tip into your lunchbox.

2 Combine the dressing ingredients in a small jar or container with a tight-fitting lid.

3 Pour the dressing over the salad just before serving and toss well.

RAW CAULIFLOWER TABOULEH

This is a low-carb take on the classic Levantine salad, replacing the traditional bulgur wheat with blitzed cauliflower. This salad also makes a fantastic accompaniment to grilled vegetables or meats, or in a wrap with pickles and a dollop of hummus.

¼ head of cauliflower, blitzed to coarse grains or use store-bought cauliflower 'rice'

1 Lebanese (short) cucumber, diced

2 spring onions (scallions), sliced

handful each of dill, mint and parsley, roughly chopped

handful of grape (baby plum) tomatoes, quartered

LEMON DRESSING

juice of ½ lemon

2 tablespoons extra virgin olive oil

salt and freshly ground black pepper, to taste

1. Toss the salad ingredients together, then tip into your lunchbox.

2. Combine the dressing ingredients in a small jar or container with a tight-fitting lid.

3. Pour the dressing over the salad just before serving and toss well.

NOODLES

+

ZOODLES

JAPANESE EDAMAME & ZOODLE SALAD

A fantastic alternative to a classic soba noodle salad, zoodles are the perfect vehicle for light and fresh Japanese flavours. To save a bit of time, you can buy frozen shelled edamame beans, which only take a few minutes to cook.

200 g (7 oz) spiralised zucchini (courgette)

1 Lebanese (short) cucumber, diced

100 g (3½ oz) cooked edamame beans

3 spring onions (scallions), thinly sliced

1 tablespoon black sesame seeds

SESAME & GINGER DRESSING

½ teaspoon sesame oil

1 tablespoon rice wine vinegar

1 tablespoon soy sauce or tamari

1 teaspoon minced ginger

1 Toss the salad ingredients together, then tip into your lunchbox.

2 Combine the dressing ingredients in a small jar or container with a tight-fitting lid.

3 Pour the dressing over the salad just before serving and toss well.

VIETNAMESE VERMICELLI NOODLE SALAD

This recipe uses fish sauce, but can easily be made vegan by substituting vegan fish sauce. There are many different versions available from health food shops and Asian grocers, generally made from ingredients, such as mushroom, soy and seaweed.

1 tablespoon salted roasted peanuts, chopped

80 g (2¾ oz) cooked vermicelli noodles, cooled under running water, drained

large handful of shredded carrot

1 spring onion (scallion), thinly sliced

50 g (1¾ oz) snow peas (mangetout), sliced

1 small Lebanese (short) cucumber, diced

small handful each of coriander (cilantro) and mint leaves, roughly chopped

NUOC CHAM DRESSING

1 tablespoon fish sauce

1½ tablespoons lime juice

2 teaspoons rice wine vinegar

1 teaspoon caster (superfine) sugar

½ red bird's eye chilli, deseeded and thinly sliced

½ teaspoon minced garlic

1. Place the peanuts in a small, airtight container.

2. Toss the remaining salad ingredients together, then tip into your lunchbox.

3. Combine the dressing ingredients in a small jar or container with a tight-fitting lid.

4. Pour the dressing and peanuts over the salad just before serving and toss well.

RAINBOW NOODLE SALAD

This colourful, low-carb salad is a fantastic way to get more veggies into your diet. You can mix up the ingredients to use what's in season – try red beetroot (beet) instead of golden, white cabbage instead of red, and yellow, green or red capsicum (bell pepper) instead of orange.

1 small zucchini (courgette), spiralised

1 small golden beetroot (beet), spiralised

1 small carrot, spiralised

¼ orange capsicum (bell pepper), sliced

handful of shredded red cabbage

handful of grape (baby plum) tomatoes, halved

ORANGE–MISO DRESSING

2 tablespoons orange juice

2 teaspoons white miso paste

1 teaspoon sesame oil

freshly ground black pepper, to taste

1. Toss the salad ingredients together, then tip into your lunchbox.

2. Combine the dressing ingredients in a small jar or container with a tight-fitting lid.

3. Pour the dressing over the salad just before serving and toss well.

CHICKEN SOBA NOODLE SALAD WITH SESAME DRESSING

The dressing on this salad is a lighter take on the wildly popular sesame-infused Japanese condiment known as goma, usually made with mayonnaise. You can, of course, add some kewpie mayo – just thin it out with a little water and add a little less sugar, as kewpie is quite sweet.

180 g (6½ oz) cooked soba noodles, cooled under running water, drained

sesame oil, for drizzling

100 g (3½ oz) sliced cooked chicken

1 spring onion (scallion), thinly sliced

50 g (1¾ oz) snow peas (mangetout), sliced

handful of shredded carrot

SESAME DRESSING

1 tablespoon toasted sesame seeds

1 tablespoon rice wine vinegar

1 tablespoon light soy sauce

¾ teaspoon caster (superfine) sugar

2 teaspoons sesame oil

1 Toss the soba noodles with a little sesame oil. Add the remaining salad ingredients and toss together, then tip into your lunchbox.

2 Combine the dressing ingredients in a small jar or container with a tight-fitting lid.

3 Pour the dressing over the salad just before serving and toss well.

CHILLI & LIME TUNA NOODLE SALAD

~~~~~~~

This fresh and summery salad uses the chilli oil from
the tuna tin as part of the dressing. If you would prefer
your salad to have less chilli, you can drain the tuna
and use a little extra virgin olive oil instead.

◇◇◇◇◇◇◇◇◇◇

95 g (3¼ oz) tin tuna in chilli
oil, undrained

150 g (5½ oz) instant ramen
noodles, cooked, cooled under
running water, drained

large handful of baby English
spinach leaves

1 celery stalk, sliced

freshly ground black pepper,
to taste

lime wedges

1. Toss the salad ingredients together,
   except the lime wedges, then tip into
   your lunchbox.

2. Squeeze the lime wedges over the
   salad just before serving and toss well.

ZOODLE PESTO SALAD

This dish is like a classic Italian pasta in salad
form. There's no need to pre-cook the zoodles,
as they marinate in the lemon juice and salt.

2 tablespoons homemade or
store-bought basil pesto

juice of 1 lemon

pinch of salt

250 g (9 oz) spiralised zucchini
(courgettes)

handful of grape (baby plum)
tomatoes, halved

freshly ground black pepper,
to taste

small handful of basil leaves,
larger leaves roughly chopped

1 Place the pesto in a small,
airtight container.

2 Massage the lemon juice and salt
into the zoodles, then gently stir
in the remaining ingredients. Tip
into your lunchbox.

3 Stir the pesto through the salad just
before serving and toss well.

BROCCOLINI & SESAME SOBA NOODLE SALAD

Simple to make, yet packed with flavour, this salad is best when broccolini is in season. If it's unavailable, just use broccoli instead.

◇◇◇◇◇◇◇◇◇◇◇

1 bunch broccolini, cut into 5 cm (2 in) lengths

180 g (6½ oz) cooked soba noodles, cooled under running water, drained

2 spring onions (scallions), thinly sliced

2 tablespoons toasted sesame seeds

HONEY SESAME DRESSING

1 teaspoon minced ginger

2 teaspoons sesame oil

1 teaspoon honey

1 tablespoon rice wine vinegar

1½ tablespoons light soy sauce

freshly ground white pepper, to taste

1. Blanch the broccolini in salted boiling water for 2 minutes. Drain and refresh under cold running water.

2. Toss the broccolini with the remaining salad ingredients, then tip into your lunchbox.

3. Combine the dressing ingredients in a small jar or container with a tight-fitting lid.

4. Pour the dressing over the salad just before serving and toss well.

SATAY CHOPPED SALAD

The satay dressing packs a flavour punch in this crunchy, summery salad. If you have dietary restrictions, crispy-fried noodles are now available in gluten-free options.

30 g (1 oz) store-bought crispy-fried noodles

large handful of shredded red cabbage

handful of shredded carrot

2 spring onions (scallions), thinly sliced

2 radishes, thinly sliced

1 red bird's eye chilli, finely chopped

small handful each of dill, mint and coriander (cilantro), roughly chopped

SATAY DRESSING

½ teaspoon minced garlic

½ teaspoon minced ginger

2 tablespoons peanut butter

2 teaspoons hoisin sauce

juice of 1 lime

1 teaspoon grated palm sugar

1 tablespoon fish sauce

salt and freshly ground white pepper, to taste

1 Place the crispy-fried noodles in an airtight container.

2 Toss the remaining salad ingredients together, then tip into your lunchbox.

3 Combine the dressing ingredients in a small jar or container with a tight-fitting lid.

4 Mix the crispy-fried noodles into the salad just before serving, pour over the dressing and toss well.

CRUNCHY RAMEN NOODLE SALAD

Adding the noodles to the salad in the morning gives them a chance to soften a little. If you want your salad to be super crunchy, leave the noodles in the packet and toss them through just before you eat.

30 g (1 oz/¼ cup) slivered almonds

85 g (3 oz) instant (ramen) noodles, broken into pieces

80 g (2¾ oz) shredded wombok (Chinese cabbage)

handful of shredded carrot

1 spring onion (scallion), thinly sliced

1 tablespoon black sesame seeds

SESAME SOY DRESSING

1 tablespoon light soy sauce

1 teaspoon sesame oil

1 teaspoon black vinegar

1 tablespoon grapeseed or other neutral-flavoured oil

½ teaspoon sugar

½ teaspoon minced ginger

1. Toss the salad ingredients together, then tip into your lunchbox.

2. Combine the dressing ingredients in a small jar or container with a tight-fitting lid.

3. Pour the dressing over the salad just before serving and toss well.

GRAINS

+

SEEDS

CALIFORNIA SUPERFOOD SALAD

Puffed wild rice brings a fantastic crunch to this salad. It can be purchased from health food stores or other specialty retailers.

75 g (2¾ oz) cooked and cooled quinoa

75 g (2¾ oz) drained tinned black beans

75 g (2¾ oz) drained tinned sweet corn kernels

handful of mixed red and yellow grape (baby plum) tomatoes, halved

handful of baby kale

1 tablespoon goji berries

1 tablespoon puffed wild rice

2 tablespoons finely grated parmesan

LIME & JALAPEÑO DRESSING

3–4 pickled jalapeño slices, finely chopped

2 tablespoons lime juice

1 tablespoon extra virgin olive oil

¼ teaspoon minced garlic

salt and freshly ground black pepper, to taste

1 Toss the salad ingredients together, then tip into your lunchbox.

2 Combine the dressing ingredients in a small jar or container with a tight-fitting lid.

3 Pour the dressing over the salad just before serving and toss well.

CHICKEN & QUINOA SALAD WITH SALSA VERDE DRESSING

A riot of green with so many fresh herbs. The salsa verde dressing is an excellent sauce – try it with steak or drizzled over roast vegetables.

100 g (3½ oz) shredded cooked chicken

150 g (5½ oz/1 cup) cooked and cooled quinoa

1 spring onion (scallion), sliced

1 celery stalk, sliced

¼ green chilli, thinly sliced

2 radishes, quartered

30 g (1 oz) toasted pine nuts

SALSA VERDE DRESSING

small handful each of basil, mint and parsley, very finely chopped

½ teaspoon minced garlic

1 tablespoon white wine vinegar

2 tablespoons extra virgin olive oil

salt and freshly ground black pepper, to taste

1. Toss the salad ingredients together, then tip into your lunchbox.

2. Combine the dressing ingredients in a small jar or container with a tight-fitting lid.

3. Pour the dressing over the salad just before serving and toss well.

MEDITERRANEAN COUSCOUS SALAD

Preserved lemon brings a real summery brightness to this salad. If you have a little more time, try making this salad with mograbieh – a larger variety of couscous, also known as pearl couscous.

150 g (5½ oz/1 cup) cooked and cooled couscous

¼ red capsicum (bell pepper), diced

½ small Lebanese (short) cucumber, diced

handful of grape (baby plum) tomatoes, halved

large handful of pitted black olives

small handful of capers, rinsed and drained

small handful of parsley, roughly chopped

PRESERVED LEMON DRESSING

¼ preserved lemon, skin only, very finely chopped

juice of ½ lemon

1 teaspoon honey

1½ teaspoons dijon mustard

2 tablespoons extra virgin olive oil

salt and freshly ground black pepper, to taste

1 Toss the salad ingredients together, then tip into your lunchbox.

2 Combine the dressing ingredients in a small jar or container with a tight-fitting lid.

3 Pour the dressing over the salad just before serving and toss well.

HOT-SMOKED TROUT, QUINOA & WATERCRESS SALAD

The peppery heat of the horseradish brings a wonderfully sophisticated bite to this salad. If you can't find hot-smoked trout, salmon will do just as well.

75 g (2¾ oz) flaked hot-smoked trout

150 g (5½ oz/1 cup) cooked and cooled quinoa

large handful of watercress, tough stalks removed

½ small Lebanese (short) cucumber, diced

juice of ½ lemon

CREAMY HORSERADISH DRESSING

2 teaspoons prepared horseradish

juice of 1 lemon

2 teaspoons baby capers

1 tablespoon crème fraîche or yoghurt

1 tablespoon extra virgin olive oil

salt and freshly ground black pepper, to taste

1 Toss the salad ingredients together, then tip into your lunchbox.

2 Combine the dressing ingredients in a small jar or container with a tight-fitting lid.

3 Pour the dressing over the salad just before serving.

BROWN RICE & HERB SALAD

~~~~~

This salad is a great way to use up left-over brown rice. If you don't have leftovers you can pre-cook some rice the night before, or use microwavable brown rice – just make sure the rice is cold before you mix in the remaining salad ingredients.

◇◇◇◇◇◇◇◇◇◇

150 g (5½ oz/1 cup) cooked and cooled brown rice

handful each of dill, parsley, coriander (cilantro) and mint, roughly chopped

2 spring onions (scallions), thinly sliced

40 g (1½ oz/¼ cup) raw almonds, roughly chopped

3 tablespoons currants

1 tablespoon each sunflower seeds and pepitas (pumpkin seeds)

LEMON & VINEGAR DRESSING

juice of ½ lemon

1 tablespoon apple cider vinegar

2 tablespoons extra virgin olive oil

salt and freshly ground black pepper, to taste

1. Toss the salad ingredients together, then tip into your lunchbox.

2. Combine the dressing ingredients in a small jar or container with a tight-fitting lid.

3. Pour the dressing over the salad just before serving and toss well.

CHICKEN & PEACH BULGUR SALAD WITH MAPLE DRESSING

In this recipe, the bulgur soaks in the time between preparing your salad in the morning and eating it at lunchtime. If you have a little more time (and you'd rather not take an extra jar with you), cover the bulgur with just-boiled water and allow to stand for 10–15 minutes before fluffing and adding to the salad.

45 g (1½ oz/¼ cup) bulgur

60 ml (2 fl oz/¼ cup) just-boiled chicken stock or water

30 g (1 oz) toasted pecans, chopped

1 ripe peach, sliced

1 teaspoon lime juice

100 g (3½ oz) shredded cooked chicken

30 g (1 oz) crumbled feta

small handful of basil leaves

MAPLE DRESSING

1½ teaspoons pure maple syrup

1 tablespoon apple cider vinegar

1 teaspoon dijon mustard

2 tablespoons extra virgin olive oil

salt and freshly ground black pepper, to taste

1. Place the bulgur in a jar or heatproof container with a tight-fitting lid. Pour in the stock or water and cover with the lid.

2. Place the pecans in a small, airtight container.

3. Toss the peach in the lime juice. Add the remaining salad ingredients and toss together, then tip into your lunchbox.

4. Combine the dressing ingredients in a small jar or container with a tight-fitting lid.

5. Before serving, fluff the bulgur with a fork and add to the salad along with the pecans and the dressing. Toss well.

CHICKEN & COUSCOUS SALAD WITH POMEGRANATE & FETA

This recipe calls for frozen pomegranate seeds for the sake of convenience, but you can definitely use fresh seeds if you have them. To save some prep time, remove the seeds from the pomegranate and store in the fridge in an airtight container for up to 3 days.

◇◇◇◇◇◇◇◇◇◇

150 g (5½ oz/1 cup) cooked and cooled couscous

100 g (3½ oz) shredded cooked chicken

handful of frozen pomegranate seeds

30 g (1 oz/¼ cup) slivered almonds

30 g (1 oz) crumbled feta

small handful each of mint and parsley leaves, chopped

POMEGRANATE DRESSING

1 tablespoon red wine vinegar

1 teaspoon pomegranate molasses

2 tablespoons extra virgin olive oil

salt and freshly ground black pepper, to taste

1. Toss the salad ingredients together, then tip into your lunchbox.

2. Combine the dressing ingredients in a small jar or container with a tight-fitting lid.

3. Pour the dressing over the salad just before serving and toss well.

QUINOA, GRAPEFRUIT & GOLDEN BEETROOT SALAD

Pre-cooked beetroot (beet) is available at good supermarkets. Golden beetroot brings a lovely colour and sweetness to this salad, but the more common red variety works just as well. You can swap the rocket (arugula) for any peppery salad leaf.

◇◇◇◇◇◇◇◇◇◇

30 g (1 oz) goat's cheese

1 small pink grapefruit

150 g (5½ oz/1 cup) cooked and cooled quinoa

100 g (5½ oz) cooked golden beetroot (beets), chopped into chunks

large handful of rocket (arugula)

¼ red onion, thinly sliced

MAPLE DRESSING

2 teaspoons maple syrup

2 teaspoons white wine vinegar

2 tablespoons extra virgin olive oil

salt and freshly ground black pepper, to taste

1. Place the goat's cheese in a small, airtight container.

2. Segment the grapefruit over a small bowl to catch the juice.

3. Whisk together the grapefruit juice and dressing ingredients, and pour into a small jar or container with a tight-fitting lid.

4. Toss the grapefruit segments and remaining salad ingredients together, then tip into your lunchbox.

5. Pour the dressing over the salad just before serving and toss well. Dot the goat's cheese over the top and serve.

TURKISH-STYLE BULGUR SALAD

This dish – called *kisir* in Turkish – is a mildly spiced bulgur salad sweetened with pomegranate molasses. If you don't have the molasses in your pantry, lemon juice will work fine, although the salad will have a more savoury flavour.

◇◇◇◇◇◇◇◇◇◇

90 g (3 oz/½ cup) bulgur

2 teaspoons tomato paste (concentrated purée)

1 teaspoon harissa (optional)

½ onion, finely chopped

125 ml (4 fl oz/½ cup) just-boiled chicken stock or water

1 spring onion (scallion), thinly sliced

handful of grape (baby plum) tomatoes, halved

handful each of parsley and mint leaves, roughly chopped

POMEGRANATE DRESSING

1 teaspoon pomegranate molasses

juice of ½ lemon

2 tablespoons extra virgin olive oil

salt and freshly ground black pepper, to taste

1. Combine the bulgur, tomato paste, harissa (if using) and onion in a jar or heatproof container with a tight-fitting lid. Pour in the stock or water and cover with the lid.

2. Place the remaining salad ingredients in your lunchbox.

3. Combine the dressing ingredients in a small jar or container with a tight-fitting lid.

4. Before serving, fluff the bulgur with a fork and add to the salad along with the dressing. Toss well.

BROWN RICE, CRANBERRY & ROSEMARY SALAD

This is a very hearty salad that's perfect for colder weather. The combination of textures here is fantastic, with the toothsome rice, chewy cranberries and crunchy roasted almonds.

juice of ½ lemon

½ apple, thinly sliced

150 g (5½ oz/1 cup) cooked and cooled brown rice

1 teaspoon finely chopped rosemary leaves

1 tablespoon dried cranberries

2 tablespoons chopped roasted almonds

handful of rocket (arugula)

MAPLE DRESSING

2 teaspoons maple syrup

1 tablespoon apple cider vinegar

1 tablespoon extra virgin olive oil

salt and freshly ground black pepper, to taste

1 Squeeze the lemon juice over the apple and toss to combine. Toss through the remaining salad ingredients, then tip into your lunchbox.

2 Combine the dressing ingredients in a small jar or container with a tight-fitting lid.

3 Pour the dressing over the salad just before serving and toss well.

BEANS

+

LEGUMES

LENTIL, HALOUMI & HERB SALAD

The haloumi brings a wonderful savoury saltiness
to this salad, but if you want to save a little time
you can substitute ricotta salata (salted ricotta) –
or even just some good-quality fresh ricotta.

◇◇◇◇◇◇◇◇◇◇

50 g (1¾ oz) slice of haloumi,
fried in hot oil for 3 minutes,
cubed

150 g (5½ oz/⅔ cup) drained
tinned brown lentils

1 tomato, diced

handful each of mint, parsley and
coriander (cilantro), chopped

LEMON & CUMIN DRESSING

juice of ½ lemon

1 teaspoon ground cumin

2 tablespoons extra virgin olive oil

salt and freshly ground black
pepper, to taste

1. Toss the salad ingredients together,
   then tip into your lunchbox.

2. Combine the dressing ingredients in
   a small jar or container with a tight-
   fitting lid.

3. Pour the dressing over the salad just
   before serving and toss well.

TUNA, CANNELLINI BEANS, GOJI & KALE SALAD

Use baby kale for this recipe, as the larger leaves can be a little tough and bitter to eat raw. If unavailable, you can substitute any green leafy vegetable, such as English spinach leaves.

100 g (3½ oz) drained tinned cannellini (lima) beans

95 g (3¼ oz) tin tuna in oil, drained

3 tablespoons goji berries

2 tablespoons grated parmesan

handful of baby kale leaves

CIDER VINEGAR DRESSING

1½ tablespoons apple cider vinegar

½ teaspoon dijon mustard

½ teaspoon honey

2 tablespoons extra virgin olive oil

salt and freshly ground black pepper, to taste

1. Toss the salad ingredients together, then tip into your lunchbox.

2. Combine the dressing ingredients in a small jar or container with a tight-fitting lid.

3. Pour the dressing over the salad just before serving and toss well.

CHICKPEA CHOPPED SALAD

~~~~~

The chickpeas (garbanzo beans) make this a deliciously hearty
lunch, but this recipe works brilliantly with any legume, so
feel free to substitute cannellini (lima) or borlotti (cranberry)
beans, or lentils – whatever you have on hand in your pantry.

◇◇◇◇◇◇◇◇◇◇

100 g (3½ oz) drained tinned
chickpeas (garbanzo beans)

1 small Lebanese (short)
cucumber, diced

¼ green capsicum (bell pepper),
diced

¼ red onion, thinly sliced

handful of grape (baby plum)
tomatoes

30 g (1 oz) crumbled feta

handful of parsley, finely chopped

OREGANO & PAPRIKA DRESSING

juice of ½ lemon

pinch of dried oregano

pinch of smoked paprika

2 tablespoons extra virgin olive oil

salt and freshly ground black
pepper, to taste

1 Toss the salad ingredients together,
then tip into your lunchbox.

2 Combine the dressing ingredients in
a small jar or container with a tight-
fitting lid.

3 Pour the dressing over the salad just
before serving and toss well.

CHIPOTLE BLACK BEAN NACHO SALAD

This salad is just like eating a bowl of nachos – but without the guilt! Look for good-quality tortilla chips at Latin grocers or in the Mexican section of your supermarket.

50 g (1¾ oz) tortilla chips

150 g (5½ oz) drained tinned black beans

75 g (2¾ oz) drained tinned sweet corn kernels

½ green capsicum (bell pepper), diced

2 spring onions (scallions), thinly sliced

½ teaspoon salt

juice of ½ lime

handful of coriander (cilantro), chopped

CHIPOTLE DRESSING

¼ teaspoon minced garlic

2 teaspoons chipotle in adobo hot sauce

juice of ½ lime

2 tablespoons sour cream

salt and freshly ground black pepper, to taste

1. Place the tortilla chips in an airtight container.

2. Toss the remaining salad ingredients together, then tip into your lunchbox.

3. Combine the dressing ingredients in a small jar or container with a tight-fitting lid.

4. Pour the dressing over the salad just before serving and use the tortilla chips to scoop up the bean mixture.

LENTIL, BEETROOT & FETA SALAD

~~~~~~

Pre-cooked beetroot (beet) is available in vacuum-
sealed packs from the supermarket. Look for
varieties with no added sugar or preservatives.

◇◇◇◇◇◇◇◇◇◇

4 cooked baked beetroot (beets),
quartered

1 Lebanese (short) cucumber,
halved lengthways and sliced

150 g (5½ oz/⅔ cup) drained
tinned brown lentils

30 g (1 oz) crumbled feta

handful each of mint and baby
English spinach leaves

BALSAMIC DRESSING

1 tablespoon balsamic vinegar

1 teaspoon dijon mustard

2 tablespoons extra virgin olive oil

salt and freshly ground black
pepper, to taste

1 Toss the salad ingredients together,
then tip into your lunchbox.

2 Combine the dressing ingredients in
a small jar or container with a tight-
fitting lid.

3 Pour the dressing over the salad just
before serving and toss well.

TUNA, CHICKPEA & CAPER SALAD

~~~~~

The sweet and salty capers take this salad to another
level. Feel free to throw in any herbs you have on hand
to add some more colour to this hearty salad.

◇◇◇◇◇◇◇◇◇◇

95 g (3¼ oz) tin tuna in oil,
drained

100 g (3½ oz) drained tinned
chickpeas (garbanzo beans)

¼ red onion, thinly sliced

2 tablespoons finely grated
parmesan

large handful of shredded
iceberg lettuce

1 tablespoon baby capers

1 tablespoon chopped dill

RED WINE VINEGAR DRESSING

1 tablespoon red wine vinegar

2 tablespoons extra virgin olive oil

salt and freshly ground black
pepper, to taste

1 Toss the salad ingredients together,
then tip into your lunchbox.

2 Combine the dressing ingredients in
a small jar or container with a tight-
fitting lid.

3 Pour the dressing over the salad just
before serving and toss well.

CORN & BEAN SALAD WITH LIME DRESSING

If you have a little more time to make this salad, chargrill a fresh corn cob instead of using tinned sweet corn. Slice off the kernels and add to your lunchbox with the remaining salad ingredients.

75 g (2¾ oz) drained tinned sweet corn kernels

100 g (3½ oz) drained tinned cannellini (lima) beans

handful of grape (baby plum) tomatoes

2 spring onions (scallions), sliced

1 tablespoon grated parmesan

handful each of mixed salad greens and torn basil leaves

LIME DRESSING

juice of ½ lime

2 tablespoons extra virgin olive oil

salt and freshly ground black pepper, to taste

1. Toss the salad ingredients together, then tip into your lunchbox.

2. Combine the dressing ingredients in a small jar or container with a tight-fitting lid.

3. Pour the dressing over the salad just before serving and toss well.

LENTIL, ZUCCHINI & MINT SALAD

~~~~~~

You can try goat's cheese in this recipe instead of the feta.
You can also mix up the herbs and use whatever you have in
your fridge or growing on your balcony or in your backyard.

◇◇◇◇◇◇◇◇◇◇

1 zucchini (courgette), cut into
ribbons using a vegetable peeler

juice of ½ lemon

pinch of salt

150 g (5½ oz/⅔ cup) drained
tinned brown lentils

large handful of mint leaves,
larger leaves chopped

small handful of parsley, chopped

30 g (1 oz) crumbled feta

2 tablespoons seeds, such as
sunflower seeds and pepitas
(pumpkin seeds)

LEMON DRESSING

zest and juice of ½ lemon

1 teaspoon white wine vinegar

2 tablespoons extra virgin olive oil

salt and freshly ground black
pepper, to taste

1 Combine the zucchini, lemon juice
and salt in a bowl. Use your hands
to massage the lemon juice into
the zucchini. Add the remaining
salad ingredients, then tip into
your lunchbox.

2 Combine the dressing ingredients in
a small jar or container with a tight-
fitting lid.

3 Pour the dressing over the salad just
before serving and toss well.

CANNELLINI BEAN & FETA SALAD

This is a simple salad that really delivers on flavour. You can use butterbeans or even chickpeas (garbanzo beans) instead of the cannellini (lima) beans.

◇◇◇◇◇◇◇◇◇◇

150 g (5½ oz) drained tinned cannellini (lima) beans

¼ red onion, thinly sliced

large handful of grape (baby plum) tomatoes

50 g (1¾ oz/⅓ cup) crumbled feta

small handful of parsley, roughly chopped

LEMON & GARLIC DRESSING

½ teaspoon minced garlic

juice of ½ lemon

2 teaspoons apple cider vinegar

1½ tablespoons extra virgin olive oil

salt and freshly ground black pepper, to taste

1. Toss the salad ingredients together, then tip into your lunchbox.

2. Combine the dressing ingredients in a small jar or container with a tight-fitting lid.

3. Pour the dressing over the salad just before serving and toss well.

CLASSICS
+ NEW
CLASSICS

CAPRESE

Treat yourself to some good-quality fresh buffalo mozzarella for this salad or, for a simpler option, use a few bocconcini balls instead.

◇◇◇◇◇◇◇◇◇◇

1 buffalo mozzarella ball, roughly torn

large handful of basil leaves, roughly torn

large handful of mixed red and yellow grape (baby plum) tomatoes

large handful of rocket (arugula)

BALSAMIC DRESSING

1 tablespoon balsamic vinegar

2 tablespoons extra virgin olive oil

salt and freshly ground black pepper, to taste

1. Toss the salad ingredients together, then tip into your lunchbox.

2. Combine the dressing ingredients in a small jar or container with a tight-fitting lid.

3. Pour the dressing over the salad just before serving and toss well.

THE NEW GREEK SALAD

A classic combination of flavours that's hard to beat.
When tomatoes are in season, try replacing the
grape tomatoes with some heirloom varieties.

large handful of grape (baby plum)
tomatoes

1 Lebanese (short) cucumber,
diced

¼ yellow capsicum (bell pepper),
diced

¼ red onion, thinly sliced

handful of pitted Kalamata olives

50 g (1¾ oz/⅓ cup) crumbled feta

1 teaspoon dried oregano

GREEK DRESSING

1 tablespoon white wine vinegar

2 tablespoons extra virgin olive oil

salt and freshly ground black
pepper, to taste

1. Toss the salad ingredients together,
then tip into your lunchbox.

2. Combine the dressing ingredients in
a small jar or container with a tight-
fitting lid.

3. Pour the dressing over the salad just
before serving and toss well.

CHICKEN FATTOUSH WITH TAHINI-YOGHURT DRESSING

This salad is a great way to use up leftovers if you've made souvlakis or wraps for dinner the night before. Pita breads can be toasted ahead of time, broken into chips and kept in an airtight container (they also make a delicious snack!).

◇◇◇◇◇◇◇◇◇◇

1 pita bread

olive oil, for brushing

sumac, for sprinkling

100 g (3½ oz) shredded cooked chicken

1 baby cos (romaine) lettuce, chopped

large handful of grape (baby plum) tomatoes, halved

small handful each of mint and parsley leaves, chopped

TAHINI-YOGHURT DRESSING

1 tablespoon each lemon juice, tahini and Greek yoghurt

1 teaspoon honey

2 teaspoons water

salt and freshly ground black pepper, to taste

1 Lightly brush the pita bread with olive oil, sprinkle with sumac, then quickly toast until golden. Set aside to cool, then break into pieces and place in a small, airtight container.

2 Toss the remaining salad ingredients together, then tip into your lunchbox.

3 Combine the dressing ingredients in a small jar or container with a tight-fitting lid.

4 Pour the dressing over the salad and toss through the pita bread just before serving.

PLOUGHMAN'S SALAD

～～～

Find yourself a nice sharp cheddar and some good-quality pickled onions for this ingenious salad. Alternatively, substitute the cheddar for a ripe blue cheese and use pear instead of apple for a twist on the classic.

◇◇◇◇◇◇◇◇◇◇

½ apple, thinly sliced

1 teaspoon lemon juice

50 g (1¾ oz) cheddar, cut into small cubes

1 celery stalk, sliced

2 radishes, thinly sliced

handful of grape (baby plum) tomatoes, halved

4 cos (romaine) lettuce leaves, roughly chopped

6 cocktail pickled onions, halved

HOT MUSTARD DRESSING

½ teaspoon hot English mustard

1 tablespoon apple cider vinegar

2 tablespoons extra virgin olive oil

salt and freshly ground black pepper, to taste

1 Toss the apple in the lemon juice. Add the remaining salad ingredients and toss together, then tip into your lunchbox.

2 Combine the dressing ingredients in a small jar or container with a tight-fitting lid.

3 Pour the dressing over the salad just before serving and toss well.

ROAST BEEF & ZUCCHINI SALAD WITH SMOKED ALMONDS

The smoked almonds give this salad a lovely flavour that pairs so well with the roast beef. You can buy smoked almonds from most good supermarkets, but you can easily substitute plain roasted almonds. This recipe is great with roast beef from your deli, but even better made with leftovers from a Sunday roast.

◇◇◇◇◇◇◇◇◇◇

30 g (1 oz) smoked almonds, chopped

1 small zucchini (courgette), cut into ribbons using a vegetable peeler

1 teaspoon lemon juice

100 g (3½ oz) sliced roast beef, torn into pieces

large handful of grape (baby plum) tomatoes, halved

handful of parsley leaves, chopped

LEMON & CHILLI DRESSING

pinch of dried chilli flakes

juice of ½ lemon

1 teaspoon dijon mustard

2 tablespoons extra virgin olive oil

salt and freshly ground black pepper, to taste

1 Place the almonds in a small, airtight container.

2 Toss the zucchini ribbons in the lemon juice. Add the remaining salad ingredients and toss together, then tip into your lunchbox.

3 Combine the dressing ingredients in a small jar or container with a tight-fitting lid.

4 Pour the dressing over the salad and toss through the almonds just before serving.

PANZANELLA

~~~~~~

A classic Italian salad designed to avoid wasting good bread after it has gone stale. Dress this salad in the morning when you're preparing it – or at least 30 minutes before eating – to give the bread some time to soak up all the delicious flavours.

◇◇◇◇◇◇◇◇◇◇

50 g (1¾ oz) stale sourdough or other crusty bread, torn or cut into bite-sized pieces

¼ red onion, thinly sliced

100 g (3½ oz) mixed ripe tomatoes, chopped

1 small Lebanese (short) cucumber, diced

handful of basil leaves, torn

VINEGAR & GARLIC DRESSING

1½ tablespoons red wine vinegar

½ teaspoon minced garlic

2 tablespoons extra virgin olive oil

salt and freshly ground black pepper, to taste

1 Place the dressing ingredients in a small jar and mix well.

2 Toss the salad ingredients together. Drizzle with the dressing and toss to combine, then tip into your lunchbox.

CHICKEN TACO SALAD WITH JALAPEÑO CREMA

Tex-Mex in salad form! Queso fresco is a mild-flavoured Mexican cheese, available at Latin grocers and some good supermarkets. You can use any cheese you like, but mild feta is the closest substitute if queso fresco is unavailable.

handful of tortilla chips, roughly broken

½ avocado, diced

juice of ½ lime

100 g (3½ oz) shredded cooked chicken

75 g (2¾ oz) drained tinned sweet corn kernels

large handful of grape (baby plum) tomatoes, halved

30 g (1 oz) queso fresco, crumbled

small handful of coriander (cilantro), roughly chopped

JALAPEÑO CREMA DRESSING

1 tablespoon lime juice

1 tablespoon Greek yoghurt

3 slices pickled jalapeños, finely chopped

salt and freshly ground black pepper, to taste

1 Place the tortilla chips in a small, airtight container.

2 Toss the avocado in the lime juice. Add the remaining salad ingredients, then tip into your lunchbox.

3 Combine the dressing ingredients in a small jar or container with a tight-fitting lid.

4 Pour the dressing over the salad just before serving and toss through the tortilla chips.

VIETNAMESE CHICKEN COLESLAW

Crispy-fried shallots are available in big packets at Asian grocers. They're fantastic to have on hand in your pantry, as they make a quick, crunchy addition to salads and noodle dishes.

◇◇◇◇◇◇◇◇◇◇

1 tablespoon chopped roasted peanuts

1 tablespoon crispy-fried shallots

100 g (3½ oz) shredded cooked chicken

handful of shredded carrot

large handful of shredded white cabbage

small handful of bean sprouts

small handful each of mint and coriander (cilantro) leaves, chopped

NUOC CHAM DRESSING

1 tablespoon fish sauce

1½ tablespoons lime juice

2 teaspoons rice wine vinegar

1 teaspoon caster (superfine) sugar

½ red bird's eye chilli, deseeded and thinly sliced

½ teaspoon minced garlic

1 Place the peanuts and shallots in a small, airtight container.

2 Toss the remaining salad ingredients together, then tip into your lunchbox.

3 Combine the dressing ingredients in a small jar or container with a tight-fitting lid.

4 Pour the dressing over the salad just before serving and toss through the peanuts and shallots.

NIÇOISE

To save yourself some time, hard-boil a few eggs at the start of the week, so you have them on hand for whipping up this quick salad. Hard-boiled eggs will keep in the fridge for up to a week.

100 g (3½ oz) blanched green beans

95 g (3¼ oz) tin tuna in spring water

¼ red onion, thinly sliced

handful of grape (baby plum) tomatoes, halved

small handful of pitted black olives

1 hard-boiled egg, halved

3 anchovy fillets, chopped (optional)

salt and freshly ground black pepper, to taste

FRENCH DRESSING

1 tablespoon red wine vinegar

2 tablespoons extra virgin olive oil

1. Toss the salad ingredients together, then tip into your lunchbox.

2. Combine the dressing ingredients in a small jar or container with a tight-fitting lid.

3. Pour the dressing over the salad just before serving and toss well.

CHINESE SILKEN TOFU SALAD

Silken tofu can be quite delicate. The 'soft' variety isn't suitable for a salad as it will fall apart, so look for 'firm' or 'extra-firm'. If you prefer some heat, leave the seeds in the chilli, or add a little chilli oil to the dressing.

100 g (3½ oz) firm silken tofu, cut into cubes

1 Lebanese (short) cucumber, chopped

large handful of grape (baby plum) tomatoes

1 spring onion (scallion), chopped

2 teaspoons toasted sesame seeds

handful of bean sprouts

small handful of coriander (cilantro) leaves, chopped

CHILLI SOY DRESSING

½ teaspoon minced garlic

½ teaspoon minced ginger

1 red bird's eye chilli, deseeded, finely chopped

1½ tablespoons light soy sauce

1 teaspoon sesame oil

1 tablespoon black vinegar

½ teaspoon sugar

1. Toss the salad ingredients together, then tip into your lunchbox.

2. Combine the dressing ingredients in a small jar or container with a tight-fitting lid.

3. Pour the dressing over the salad just before serving and toss well.

PROSCIUTTO, NECTARINE & ROCKET SALAD WITH HONEY–DIJON DRESSING

This salad is a summer treat when stone fruits are in season. It works just as well with peaches, too, and why not try substituting fresh buffalo mozzarella for the parmesan for a more mellow flavour. If you have a little more time up your sleeve, the fruit is delicious chargrilled.

1 ripe nectarine, sliced

1 teaspoon lemon juice

3 slices prosciutto, torn

30 g (1 oz) shaved parmesan

large handful of rocket (arugula)

HONEY–DIJON DRESSING

1 teaspoon dijon mustard

1 teaspoon honey

juice of ½ lemon

2 tablespoons extra virgin olive oil

salt and freshly ground black pepper, to taste

1. Toss the nectarine in the lemon juice. Add the remaining salad ingredients and toss together, then tip into your lunchbox.

2. Combine the dressing ingredients in a small jar or container with a tight-fitting lid.

3. Pour the dressing over the salad just before serving and toss well.

PRAWN COCKTAIL SALAD

Don't knock this deconstructed '80s classic until you've tried it. It's filling, nutritious and delicious!

juice of ½ lemon

1 avocado, diced

150 g (5½ oz) cooked peeled prawns (shrimp)

handful of shredded iceberg lettuce

1 Lebanese (short) cucumber, chopped

salt and freshly ground black pepper, to taste

MARIE-ROSE DRESSING

1½ tablespoons whole-egg mayonnaise

1 tablespoon tomato ketchup

1 tablespoon lemon juice

dash of Tabasco sauce, to taste

1. Squeeze the lemon juice over the avocado and gently toss to combine. Toss through the remaining salad ingredients, then tip into your lunchbox.

2. Combine the dressing ingredients in a small jar or container with a tight-fitting lid.

3. Pour the dressing over the salad just before serving and toss well.

RAW PAD THAI

This recipe is a fantastic low-carb alternative to the classic Thai dish. Save time by using pre-cut vegetables and a store-bought Thai-style dressing.

½ carrot, spiralised or grated

¼ red capsicum (bell pepper), thinly sliced

1 Lebanese (short) cucumber, sliced

50 g (1¾ oz) snow peas (mangetout), trimmed and sliced

2 spring onions (scallions), thinly sliced

handful of bean sprouts

small handful of unsalted peanuts, roughly chopped

TAMARIND DRESSING

½ teaspoon minced garlic

½ teaspoon minced ginger

1 tablespoon tamarind purée

juice of ½ lime

2 teaspoons fish sauce

2 teaspoons caster (superfine) sugar

1. Toss the salad ingredients together, then tip into your lunchbox.

2. Combine the dressing ingredients in a small jar or container with a tight-fitting lid.

3. Pour the dressing over the salad just before serving and toss well.

CHICKEN, MANGO & JALAPEÑO SALAD

The spicy kick in the jalapeño dressing perfectly balances the sweetness of the mango. Unlike many other fruits, mango doesn't brown after it has been cut, so you can dice your mango ahead of time and store in an airtight container in the fridge for up to 4 days.

◇◇◇◇◇◇◇◇◇◇

100 g (3½ oz) shredded cooked chicken

½ ripe mango, diced

1 baby cos (romaine) lettuce, chopped

¼ red capsicum (bell pepper), diced

small handful of coriander (cilantro), roughly chopped

JALAPEÑO DRESSING

juice of ½ lime

3 pickled jalapeño slices, finely chopped

1 tablespoon extra virgin olive oil

salt and freshly ground black pepper, to taste

1 Toss the salad ingredients together, then tip into your lunchbox.

2 Combine the dressing ingredients in a small jar or container with a tight-fitting lid.

3 Pour the dressing over the salad just before serving and toss well.

INDEX

Raw brussels sprouts with pear, hazelnuts & pecorino 20
Raw cauliflower tabouleh 30
Raw pad thai 120
Red wine vinegar dressing 86

Rice
Brown rice & herb salad 62
Brown rice, cranberry & rosemary salad 72
California superfood salad 54

Ricotta
Baby beetroot, walnut & ricotta salad 12
Spring vegetable salad with lemony ricotta 26
Roast beef & zucchini salad with smoked almonds 104

Rocket (arugula)
Broccoli rice, carrot & cranberry salad with buttermilk dressing 14
Caprese 96
Prosciutto, nectarine & rocket salad with honey–dijon dressing 116
Quinoa, grapefruit & golden beetroot salad 68

Rosemary
Brown rice, cranberry & rosemary salad 72

Salsa verde dressing 56
Satay chopped salad 48
Satay dressing 48
Scallions, see spring onions

Seeds
Broccolini & sesame soba noodle salad 46
Brown rice & herb salad 62
Chicken soba noodle salad with sesame dressing 40
Chinese silken tofu salad 114
Crunchy ramen noodle salad 50
Japanese edamame & zoodle salad 34
Korean bibimbap salad with kimchi dressing 18
Lentil, zucchini & mint salad 90
Shredded beetroot, dill & mustard seed salad 28
Sesame & ginger dressing 34
Sesame dressing 40
Sesame soy dressing 50
Shredded beetroot, dill & mustard seed salad 28
Shrimp, see prawns
Som tum 24

Sour cream
Chipotle black bean nacho salad 82

Spinach
Chilli & lime tuna noodle salad 42
Left-over roast vegetable salad 22
Lentil, beetroot & feta salad 84
Roast baby beetroot, walnut & ricotta salad 12

Spring onions (scallions)
Broccolini & sesame soba noodle salad 46
Brown rice & herb salad 62

Chicken & quinoa salad with salsa verde dressing 56
Chicken soba noodle salad with sesame dressing 40
Chinese silken tofu salad 114
Chipotle black bean nacho salad 82
Corn & bean salad with lime dressing 88
Crunchy ramen noodle salad 50
Japanese edamame & zoodle salad 34
Korean bibimbap salad with kimchi dressing 18
Raw cauliflower tabouleh 30
Raw pad Thai 120
Satay chopped salad 48
Turkish-style bulgur salad 70
Vietnamese vermicelli noodle salad 36
Spring vegetable salad with lemony ricotta 26

Sweet potato
Left-over roast vegetable salad 22

Tahini
Chicken fattoush with tahini–yoghurt dressing 100
Left-over roast vegetable salad 22
Tahini dressing 22
Tahini–yoghurt dressing 100
Tamarind dressing 120
The new greek salad 98

Tofu
Chinese silken tofu salad 114

Tomatoes
California superfood salad 54
Cannellini bean & feta salad 92
Caprese 96
Chicken fattoush with tahini–yoghurt dressing 100
Chicken taco salad with jalapeño crema 108
Chickpea chopped salad 80
Chinese silken tofu salad 114
Corn & bean salad with lime dressing 88
Lentil, haloumi & herb salad 76
Mediterranean couscous salad 58
Niçoise 112
Panzanella 106
Ploughman's salad 102
Prawn cocktail salad 118
Rainbow noodle salad 38
Raw cauliflower tabouleh 30
Roast beef & zucchini salad with smoked almonds 104
Som tum 24
The new Greek salad 98
Turkish-style bulgur salad 70
Zoodle pesto salad 44
Tuna, cannellini beans, goji & kale salad 78
Tuna, chickpea & caper salad 86
Tuna, see fish & seafood
Turkish-style bulgur salad 70

Vegan
Broccolini & sesame soba noodle salad 46
Brown rice & herb salad 62
Brown rice, cranberry & rosemary salad 72
California superfood salad 54
Chinese silken tofu salad 114
Crunchy ramen noodle salad 50
Fennel & radicchio citrus salad 16
Japanese edamame & zoodle salad 34
Left-over roast vegetable salad 22
Mediterranean couscous salad 58
Panzanella 106
Rainbow noodle salad 38
Raw cauliflower tabouleh 30
Shredded beetroot, dill & mustard seed salad 28
Turkish-style bulgur salad 70
Zoodle pesto salad 44
Vietnamese chicken coleslaw 110
Vietnamese vermicelli noodle salad 36
Vinegar & garlic dressing 106

Watercress
Hot-smoked trout, quinoa & watercress salad 60
Winter squash, see pumpkin

Yoghurt
Chicken fattoush with tahini–yoghurt dressing 100
Chicken taco salad with jalapeño crema 108
Hot-smoked trout, quinoa & watercress salad 60

Zoodle pesto salad 44
Zucchini (courgette)
Japanese edamame & zoodle salad 34
Lentil, zucchini & mint salad 90
Rainbow noodle salad 38
Roast beef & zucchini salad with smoked almonds 104
Zoodle pesto salad 44

Published in 2019 by Smith Street Books
Collingwood | Melbourne | Australia
smithstreetbooks.com

ISBN: 9781925418972

CIP data is available from the National Library of Australia

Publisher: Paul McNally
Editor: Lucy Heaver, Tusk studio
Designer: Kate Barraclough
Introductory text: Hannah Koelmeyer & Patrick Boyle
Photographer: Chris Middleton
Food stylist: Deborah Kaloper

Printed & bound in Italy by L.E.G.O. S.p.A.

Book 76
10 9 8 7 6 5 4